A Nurse's Journey

Hazel McShane

A Hearthstone Book

Carlton Press Corp.　　　　　　　　　New York

Copyright © 1996 by Hazel McShane
ALL RIGHTS RESERVED
Manufactured in the United States of America
ISBN 0-8062-5015-1

A Nurse's Journey

Roaming...wandering...the simple life—if I could I'd live it again—a worthwhile life, helping and being helped.

There are many to thank, for without their contacts I would not be able to complete my script, and most of all, I have not forgotten my God, who gives me grace each day to write each line.

Sparkling Villa was what the home was called where we were born. Yes, so it was sparkling, standing out there on the hill, glittering with the rise of a new dawn, twinkling in the burning sun, glowing at sunset, nestled among the hills. The singing of birds; the nightingale, pea doves and gray-speckled wings; the chirping of the John Chewit and the sparrow; the woodpeckers and whatnot, drowned by the crowing of the cock rooster, was the music that one awoke to every morning.

The old house with its bright gleaming rooms from east to west. Mother's room was the biggest and best, for there everyone seemed to find some time to frolic, sit, and watch her make dainty dresses with frills of lace for us to wear. No one else had dresses like ours. The first two girls shared one room while the younger ones had another. The boy was by himself in a little room off the pantry with jalousie windows that Mom called louvered panels. The four-poster bed in Mother's room was the place where everyone would doze during the day. The maid's room was attached to the kitchen, a few steps away from the main building.

Stony hills and deep valleys surrounded the homestead, some of which was rarely seen during the year. A stony yard surrounded the house: the kuskus patch with its fragrant root, the sweet sap tree, a pear tree, and grapefruit and orange trees to the north. On the east was a grape arbor, Seville oranges and a kitchen garden continued on the east, while bordering on the south were tangerine trees and flowers. To think of it, the entire building was encircled with flowers of all species. Delicate plants were potted and housed under the westside veranda that Mother tended with fond delight. After her children came her flowers. The schools and colleges got their laundry baskets full of cut flowers for display and decorations on special occasions. The large barbecue that served as a catchment for the tank was also used for the drying of crops such as pimentos and coffee.

For exercise and fun we played cricket. On the lawn on about an acre of sloping ground, we rolled down the hill, skipped rope, ran sack races, and swung under the wild grape tree. Life was fun and the fun of early childhood lingered long.

It was in the early twentieth century that the green pastures became dry and parched lands, as there were months when no rain fell and the animals had to travel from one end of the farm to another for water. The three tanks (small reservoir) were at distant locations. A small bucket suspended from a rope was used to draw water to fill the cisterns for the animals to drink. The pastures were good for grazing and no one seemed to have been too worried about growing up and living free and easy; the lifestyle was casual and nothing mattered.

Everyone was now growing up, and the time for starting school came. We all started school at the age of four. In those days the only way to get to school was to walk, and those who could afford to pay for tuition went to a private school in a one-room schoolhouse. My first school was about two miles away and it was private and exclusive. The teacher, a friend of my mother, made it very hard for one to misbehave. The children were taken to school by a nursemaid. Every Monday I can remember seeing a basket of meat and vegetables being sent to the teacher, who received it graciously, because it was from that supply we were given our midday lunch which her cook prepared. Lunch was taken with the teacher at her dining table, where we sat erect and always used a knife and fork just as was practiced at home.

To get to school each day, shortcuts were taken. Our parents got permission from an English neighbor for us to walk through his property. We had five days of trotting back and forth, with the maid taking us to school and meeting us in the evening. It was rumored that bush robbers lived in caves on our neighbor's property in addition to wild cows which would try and get you. Sometimes we climbed trees to avoid them. Such fun it is now for me, remembering those times.

During the early days in school we used slate and hard slate pencils. School was great fun; we stood back to back for arithmetic and mostly all subjects. Whoever finished first took his slate to the teacher. I cannot forget the boy who copied and could not tell how he got the correct answer. It was then I was called and threatened by the teacher for holding my slate carelessly for someone to see. With that, I started to run because I had tasted of that thin leather strap before. I was caught by an older pupil and taken back for my lashes in the palm of my hand. Well, I went home and could not mention anything about my lashes, for whoever brought the news of bad behavior was punished again. We were taught to be straightforward if not brilliantly smart.

My father was a stately gentleman, who rose up early every morning to oversee the milking of the cows, and the feeding of the ducks, chickens, turkeys, and the tending of the goats, while Mammy was busy getting breakfast and getting the children ready for school. It was the business of these different activities each morning that established a worthwhile routine.

I remember my sister and I sleeping in the room next to my mother, and since I was the one who hated the smell of milk, I paid for it with early tooth decay. One night, when my first toothache started, I did not know what was going to happen to me. I flew out of the bedroom and ran to my parents' room and jumped in bed between them, trembling and crying until the ache subsided. The next morning, my father took me six miles away, both of us on horseback, to the nearest dentist, to be treated. On the way home, my horse took off when my father stopped to speak with someone. I got lost, ending up in a cul-de-sac facing a large gate. The horse knew the road as she had objected to going that way; so, we turned around. When I reached the intersection I saw my father coming up from where I started. He had started to wonder what had happened to me. We reached home together, riding along a stony pathway from Santa Cruz to Sparkling Villa. The roads were not paved, but were gravel and dirt and seldom traveled by vehicles.

School was fun. We had a choice of games; while the boys played cricket, the girls played baseball and basketball. On the days when it rained, we learned to take off our shoes and paddle along in the pools of water on the unpaved areas along the way.

Progress was great and after the first three years we used pens with steel nibs and single-line exercise books. Each student took his turn to wash and refill the inkwells. After sixth grade, the first teacher retired and left the area, so we were transferred to another private school near the Teachers Training College. The headmistress became known as Aunt Nell. She was more strict and offered a variety of technical and cultural subjects. It was in her house that we took music lessons. The lessons were scheduled for before the start of school or after lunch, which made it hard in those days. Music lessons were taught on the organ and practice was continued at home. Aunt Nell's niece would help her sometimes. She was more gentle and patient. Aunt Nell would use her baton to conduct while I felt out the notes. She often used her baton on my knuckles when a wrong note was struck or the time was wrong; one had to be prepared for her. She could be heard keeping time: 1-2-3, and so on. To our surprise, when her niece got married to one of her pupils' brothers and soon took off, Aunt Nell discontinued her private school.

It was at this time our parents were forced to look for a proper school. The nearby school was substandard. After trying it for one half year, a decision was made for everyone to travel six miles away to finish high school. This caused much confusion among the older generation as the heads of both of the local schools were our immediate relatives. One was the father and one the brother of our mother, and the other was a niece of our father. After arrangements were made, off we went, three of us on horseback over hills and valleys in rainstorms and dust. There were racing cars that caused us to be thrown from the horse when the stirrups broke, and one lost her balance when the horse became too frisky and fell over on the side of the bank. The horse would stand and look as if to say, "What did you fall over for?" Sometimes the horse would gallop on to be brought back by the others. I guess it was milk or fresh fruits and vegetables which kept us from breaking our bones. We had to take a tall glass of milk just as it was gotten from the cows every morning.

Father would get up early in the mornings to supervise or see that the cows were milked on time and the horses were properly groomed and saddled for us. Our aunt who lived next to the school took care of our lunch, and we were allowed to turn out the horses on her pasture. The younger girl rode a donkey to start (she was a large gray animal who took first prize at the agricultural show). This younger child did not like to ride the donkey and would fight for the horses.

We all learned to put on the bridle and saddle and girth the horse. Once when the oldest brown mare developed a sore back, I had to ride the stallion, a furious beast, who nickered and railed hard with the least provocation. To control him I was taught to hold up the reins, give him the stirrup and offer him the whip. That settled the beast when, I think halfway down the hill, he would shut up and ride along with the others; such fun was never heard of. The palomino mare (that is what I think she was) was a beautiful chestnut with a white streak in the middle of her head. She would amble and dance her way along with such style and grace, even on the unpaved roads and bridle paths, and was the envy of all. That accounts for the fact that everyone wanted to ride her! The horses were usually hitched under pimento trees ready and waiting for us. Whoever got out first would race for the dancer. If there was a tie, a fight started, and when it got beyond endurance, father would call out to the farmhand to go turn out the horses and command us to walk to school that morning. No one dared argue, but trotted the six horrid miles. Once this lesson was given and learned very well; on that special day we were punished before the class. We stood up that morning as "the late ones." The only thing good that day was, the sedate old aunt had cooked fresh lunch for us. I remember her with her crisp, clean gathered apron when in the kitchen, and the good stuff she would give us like honeycombs, cassava wafers, and gumbo pea soup. The cakes and corn pone, like all the food, were made from natural food with no preservatives.

Our father was softhearted, too. He could not see us walking the twelve miles in one day, so the horses were sent for us that evening. Sometime after this, another lesson was taught when the rain poured and we took shelter at the house of one of the students. We did not get home on time and the old gentleman came to look for us himself. When he found us, we were scolded for not coming straight home. Whether it was wet or dry we were not to stop at anyone's house or take shelter without permission. I graduated from high school without any honors, and actually I was happy to see the end of those days.

Once there was a terrible hurricane; we lost half the roof of the house. Yet we were able to live comfortably in the other five rooms and offer shelter to the peasants from the nearby district who had lost most of their possessions. The organ was shifted to the dining room until the repair was done. My father, Uncle Lannie, and his two nephews, Harold and Arthur, did the repairing of the damage. The day before, the preparation was made for delicious, fresh cooked ham, fresh fish, ackee and codfish, coffee and rum meal. The ceiling was put up sometime after and since my brother was away at college, it fell on me to hand up nails and boards when Pappy needed them. After the ceiling was finished, we painted it. Instead of making a shingled roof, it was done with galvanized zinc, and everyone liked it. One could hear the music of the raindrops before the shower pitter-pattering down and later pouring loudly. It was different and interesting to just sit and listen to the "rain music." The wood from the veranda was replaced with low-contoured mason cement sills wide enough to hold some of Mammy's flowerpots.

Not long after this, an application allowed me to attend nursing school. It was then that tension started, as I waited one year to be accepted. The rules and regulations were rigid. The special stripes of blue could be purchased only at one specific store. The uniforms were nine inches from the ground with mannish neck bands and long sleeves for white cuffs to match the stiff high collar. The uniforms were similar to those worn by Miss Nightingale. Black oxford shoes with rubber heels and black stockings were also part of the daily attire.

The Custos of the parish (an Englishman) said to me "Imagine you are a little girl going to study nursing." He gave me a good recommendation, not on my merit, for I did not know the man, but on the basis of my parents' standing in the district. Others were given by the minister of the church and by the headmaster of the last school. Having passed the physical, my father went with me on horseback to have my teeth filled so that I'd go into training 100% fit.

By February I got all my things together. Mammy made my dress to the specific requirements and accompanied me to the training hospital some thirty-five miles from home. The first day I got my uniform on and went in front of the mirror. I could not believe it was me looking like a little old lady. It was a good thing the uniform was long so no one could call me spindle legs.

After I was lined up on the march to start what was to be my lifelong career, I began to see life differently. The matron, a tall, masculine-looking woman, laid down the rules to the new probationers (as we were called). Breakfast at 5:30 a.m. for those who had to be on duty by 6 a.m., a fifteen-minute tea break at 10 a.m. and one half hour for lunch. We covered a full twelve-hour shift. Lights out at 10 p.m. for those who had to be up for 5:30 a.m. breakfast. We started at 6 a.m. around the night nurses' table to listen to the report of what went on during the night. Then we were taken to a small demonstration room and taught bed-making, damp dusting, bedpan handling, sluicing the bedpan, cleaning dentures, mouth care, and all the rough work connected with nursing. Work started at 6 a.m. and finished at 6 p.m. each day, with breaks for lunch, tea and supper. If one was fortunate enough, one would have every other Sunday off.

Our laundry and housecleaning were taken care of by the staff of the nurse's quarters. No one on night duty was allowed out during the day. The first year was rough and dragged on slowly. The doctors lectured us in anatomy and physiology, surgery and operating room procedure, while the matron and head nurse took turns giving lectures on nursing ethics, first aid and medical and surgical nursing.

During those years there were no nurse's aides or orderlies; such names were never thought of. The probation nurse, chiefly in her first six months of orientation, encountered and accomplished all those duties (e.g., emptied spittoon mugs, scoured bedpans and cleaned bedside tables). Porters and ward maids did the heavy work and housekeeping duties. Each ward had sterilizers and the nurse would do her own sterilization of instruments as she needed. Sometimes boiling water for poultices and fomentation was fetched by the student nurse from the main kitchen which was connected to the hospital by a long corridor. I had a spill once, hot water and myself went flying down the stairs; no one could understand how I was not scalded to death and there stood a doctor taking in the act. When I got my wits together and returned with the pitcher of boiling water, the doctor asked me, "Tell me the first thing one does after a fall?" Ignorant of the answer I replied, "Get up?"

"No," he said, "look up to see who is watching you fall."

The wards were long, each bed separated by a heavy cloth screen, with twenty or more beds in one section. Only two private rooms were on one, one for male and one for female. These were reserved for the wealthy patients. If a patient was very sick and dying, the screen around his bed was kept permanently drawn. This I learned the hard way. After six months of probation, I was to sit by the bedside of a pneumonia patient who became delusional and jumped out of bed. I took hold of him not knowing what to do, and he pulled me to the end of the ward before I was able to grab a pillar and call for help. After that experience, I felt like running away.

On another occasion I had to care for a man behind a screen, who no one told me was dying. When he gasped for breath, I ran to the sister on the floor (the head nurses were called sisters). It was then she told me that the man was dying and that someone had to witness his death, the time and the hour he died. Needless to say, this was enough to chill my spine. I went back and sat there trembling with prayers, for I had not seen anyone die before. A while later, he drew his last breath. I then got my first lesson in the care of the patient after death, including a sponge bath like the nursing procedures taught in the demonstration room on the big fat rubber doll.

For surgery, it was observation to start. The junior nurses were draped in a gown and put far down towards the foot section of the operating table to watch the surgeon at work. Some girls fainted and had to be taken out of the O.R.; thank God it wasn't me. I don't know what kept me from passing out. I found myself getting closer and closer to the operating table when I felt a tug on my gown. "Nurse, where are you going?" the supervisor asked. "You are not scrubbed."

One day I felt myself weak in the knees at the mortuary. Because I was taller than average, I was classed older and more responsible, and put in the back row of the class. I really was the youngest of the class. I got called on and was given more than I could take. I was summoned to witness an autopsy. The usual exploration went well with me, but when it came to the sawing of the skull, I excused myself and went to my room in the nurse's quarters. I thought it was a shame to be treating the dead so disgracefully. Actually I felt sick and went to my bed. When news of my absence reached the matron, she came to get me, had me up, dressed, and marched me back to the morgue. I felt like a thief and suffered in silence; there was no one to tell how horrid I felt and suffered.

My days of scrubbing and orientation soon ended. The practical and theoretical exams were near. We could do bandaging well; washing and rolling the bandages by hand; the butterfly bandage, the T bandage, and the triangular eye bandage. The hardest ones to master were the skull and stump. Despite all my horrid experiences, I was given high marks and sent home for a two-week holiday. I went home in good standing as far as the hospital was concerned, but in my heart I was praying that after I told Mother all the experiences and horrid things I had suffered, she would say, "You have had enough; you won't go back." Instead she had my uniforms and everything well laundered and packed away, saying, "If you had failed your exam you would have a reason not to go back." It was then that I felt another year like the past would sure find me dead stiff.

In March, I returned to the public hospital approximately one hundred miles away. The environment was much better. Each student nurse had her own small room, a simple bed, a dresser, closet, a bedside table and a chair, with enough room to turn around in. It made one feel more private and respectable. Then again, the evil reflections from the past year flashed through my mind. I relived them like a nightmare: falling down the stairs with the hot water, the delirious patient drawing me across the ward, watching the first dying man breath his last, the dead man in the morgue having his head sawed open, and me flying like a breeze to my room. Had the first year been different, I guess I would not be so afraid. Now we were given a white tab to wear on our arm to show that we were no longer probationers and could work alongside senior nurses and under supervision.

The second year started well and my interest grew with the thought of being helpful to those who needed someone no matter who. My assignments were supervised and I was transferred from the medical floor to the surgical, under the guidance of a stern, disciplined, half-German head nurse, who never married or even had dates and thought that no one should let a doctor look at her, much less touch her. All of the doctors knew her and respected her for her thorough guidance and excellent discipline in nursing. It was under her supervision I properly learned to do all nursing procedures and gained the admiration of many doctors and fellow nurses.

The nurse's quarters, at a two-story building located almost opposite the side entrance of the hospital, had long corridors that were the best thing to think of when one wanted to get away on a day off. Actually one was scarcely fit to do anything else on those days but rest. The curfew was at 10 p.m.; at that time all lights in the sleeping quarters and recreation room were put out. The senior night nurse assigned to this duty would come around and knock you into compliance. Not many knew the trick of being smart after the nurse had done her rounds. We would pull the night light down to the floor and cover it over with a blanket, for that was the only way one could catch up with the lecture, study, and take notes that had to be submitted to the matron for correction and evaluation. The doctors were our tutors on diseases and surgery, while the matron taught us nursing.

The second year was full of meaningful nursing encounters and seemed to have been the shortest year. I met some lonely fellow nurses, resident doctors and older men who seemed to have enjoyed all their work and encounters with us. Nurses dated doctors on their days off and went out to the theater, botanic garden agricultural shows, and sightseeing just for fun.

There was no lounging around, so not one patient stood in need of medical or nursing services. A multiplicity of demands and responsibilities crowded the third year. Suddenly we were seniors in charge of wards with fifty to ninety patients. At this stage, all student charge nurses were given five pounds a week in this high position.

We did more intensive training: lecture, pathology and surgical procedures, assisting in setting up for surgery, and dressing of surgical wounds, preparing the back for post mortem, holding the mask, and helping the pharmacist who was also a licensed anesthesiologist. After surgery it was the charge nurse who did all surgical dressings and removed sutures. The incision or suture line would be partially left open and covered for the surgeon to inspect when he did his rounds. The junior nurse would follow us around and carry a basin, soap and towel that were used as soon as one patient was attended. Life in nursing progressed interestingly, and more and more, one developed a confidence in oneself.

During the last months of the third year, I experienced real confrontations with everyone. The transfer from the surgical to the medical floors was through an underbuilding ward, as it was called, a ward housing some fifty to eighty patients, most of whom were on some sort of government aid. We had an intermixing of typhoid, malaria, measles, mumps, and other common infectious or contagious diseases. No TB patients were kept here; as soon as a case was diagnosed, the patient was transferred to a TB Sanitarium on a hill, about fifteen miles away from the general hospital.

Our typhoid fever cases were absolutely in isolation, the likes of which one can never forget. They were in small cubicles on the west side of the ward and pails of carbolic disinfectant were for their used linen. The special nurse assigned to this patient never attended anyone else. She had all the precautions and technique training in the nursing of typhoid; everything was done for the patient. Because I was in charge of this, I could see why no one enjoyed these duties, because there was an increasing complexity of changes day after day. Nearly all the emergency room cases came here first. We were near the hospital emergency room and received many detained cases.

Early one afternoon, a male patient who had worked in a convent as a caretaker of the gardens and all, was wheeled in on a stretcher. Well, he was supposed to have consumed enough Lysol to cause his death. The patient was followed by the D.O.D. who immediately gave orders, antidote and special care to be observed every fifteen minutes. When hopes were given up, everyone thought the man would have died. The next morning this special case was seen by the same doctor who admitted him; he was evaluated, and orders were given for the patient's discharge in a day or two. That same evening the patient collapsed while out of bed and was put back to bed hurriedly. I called the doctor before the doctor reached the ward (in say about fifteen minutes). The patient had ceased to breathe. I then called the priest.

When the priest got there "fireworks" began. I was reprimanded by the priest for not calling him first. I replied, "Father, the doctor is called first in these cases." The priest went straight to the matron's office and had me reported for insubordination. The telephone rang and summoned me to come to the matron's office right away to explain and write an account of what happened. I was told that no matter what, a nurse never answers her superior whether he be a doctor or a priest. That was the lesson taught. For days I lived with the thought "that I could be right."

The underbuilding was my last assignment before the final board examinations. There were thirty-seven of us girls in this batch. But before I sat for the final, I must mention some experience of night duty that each student had for at least three months each year. Of course it was different sleeping days; getting awakened at 5 p.m. for the 6 a.m. to 6 p.m. shift, which allowed an hour off at midnight or thereabouts for napping or doing whatever away from the ward in the quiet nurse's room, a cubicle off the main ward. This is where we also received reports before starting duty and at the end of each shift.

Morning duties started at 4 a.m. when all bed patients who needed it were given a partial bath, oral hygiene, back care, and sometimes change of draw sheets or entire bed linen. The night nurse was responsible for leaving her ward tidy and her patients comfortable. All temperatures taken during the night were recorded. The activities of night differed from day care in that we did not have to encounter so many doctors on the floor, and no diet trays were served. Surprise visits from the matron or night supervisor had everyone on their p's and q's.

Having done what you thought was best, one went off night duty, rolled the long sleeves down, and put white cuffs on, scrubbed thoroughly and rushed straight to the dining room, where there was breakfast: cereal, milk, eggs, coffee or tea, and fruit for those who wanted it. Then to the shower and to bed. No one got to roam around since we were always being watched, and were not disturbed unless there was a lecture or demonstration class. At 4 p.m. we were up and ready for supper, some of which we would sneak out to nibble on at break time during the night. Night nurses were expected to go straight to bed after breakfast.

On Sundays those who wanted to attend church were given a special pass the day before. Well, on this special day, a group of us decided to sin. We applied for the pass, tucked our swimsuits in our pocketbooks or handbags and took off for the beach. All was well, everything was timed to match church services; the trouble was what to do with the wet bathing suits? We could not leave them in the rooms, as these were sometimes inspected for tidiness after we left for duty. So we ended up taking them with us on duty and hanging them somewhere unnoticed to dry. Until this day no one ever found out what we did; but there was too much trouble involved, so we never did it again.

About two months after that there was an uproar in the dining room. A group of student nurses got up to leave the dining room with the midday meal they were served. The uncovered dishes with a measly helping of meat and vegetables were taken individually by six nurses brave enough to face the director of medical service and show him what was being given to them. These girls were the backbone of the hospital. They claimed they worked like brutes on the ward and were fed like rats with diets that could not support and replace what energy they expended, and as a consequence, they were losing weight and becoming weaker and weaker. This was the worst thing to have happened, but it helped in getting all of us better meals. The six nurses were reported for misbehavior and slated to see the matron at 9 a.m. the next day. The girls did not care two flies, for it was said that the student nurses got the worst of everything.

It appeared that everything was happening to teach us lessons worth remembering through our final year. There was a train wreck and all off-duty nurses were commanded to report immediately for duty. All off-duty nurses who were not residents in the quarters or were leaving the residence were required to leave their addresses where they could be reached in case of emergencies. A few of these girls could not be found and were slated to report to the matron next day. We had ambulances with patients who were in need of surgery, suturing, splinting, bandaging, and every imaginable first aid that could be applied. Most of the injured were taken directly to the various wards. Of course, the nurses met their Waterloo when they came back. Those who were fully trained had their licenses suspended for six months, and the students were relieved of duty for six months, which meant that instead of graduating with the class, they had to wait six months longer for the next graduation exercises.

For our Christmas party there was a lot of excitement. The Christmas dinner is worth remembering, for it was then the doctors got the chance to serve us. We sat down and the doctors waited at the tables. The auditorium was well polished with a platform for the musicians, and the party began after the dinner. The nurses danced, wined, and sat with their boyfriends. Those who had none were not really wallflowers, for the doctors saw to it that they had a chance to show their stuff on the dance floor. We wined and danced until midnight, and next day it was the old routine again.

Well, all things must come to an end. Thirty-seven of us sat the final exams; ten failed. I sighed a sigh of relief when this period ended, at least I could go home and wait for my certificate to practice. This was signed by the Senior Medical Office, the head of the Board of Examiners, and the matron.

After this I started to wonder what was next. I submitted my application to enter the hospital and begin training to be a maternity nurse and midwife, in the field of obstetrics and gynecology. Still at home, waiting to be called, the measles broke out in the nearby boys' boarding school. The school nurse could not cope and I was called to help.

One whole dormitory was given up as a sanitorium; the sick room had only two beds—this was the nurse's office. Nearly fifty percent of the students were infected. How I did not get the measles is a mystery. The year of '37 seemed to be a bad one. I lived in the compound during the entire epidemic. No sooner was everyone better and the quarantine lifted than I went home to be called. One of the headmasters got the measles and was confined to his home a few miles away from the college. Where he lived there was an interesting old stone bungalow with beautiful flowers around. Facing the other side of the unpaved street was the famous and exclusive golf course. I spent half my time on the veranda watching them play golf. With just one patient, there was not much nursing. I was doomed to occupy my early days in the real nursing field among the school faculty. For when the headmaster was sick, I was again called to nurse him.

The year went by quickly. There were not many qualified nurses around, only an old midwife, a relative of mine who only did the delivery of babies. While waiting to be accepted for midwifery training, I joined the staff in the rural hospital where I first started my training. I had charge of the emergency room where incised wounds, seen by the doctor on duty, were ordered to be sutured by the charge nurse. Multiple emergencies were seen. It was there that I had the opportunity to assist and instruct the police from the nearby station in the application of bandages, splints, and the transportation of the injured. I went there with the understanding that as soon as I was called to start my training in maternity nursing, I would leave. In March of the next year, I left.

Uniform specifications were similar to those of general nursing, so my apron and collars and cuffs were useful.

It was tough all over again; a full year of theory, practice, learning the differences in general nursing, the pregnant woman and childbirth. We attended lectures given by the chief of gynecology and obstetrics, studied the pelvis, the fetus in utero, and demonstrated the delivery of the baby in different positions over and over again in a large room equipped with skeletons and segments of the pelvis, the normal and the abnormal.

Each nurse was told she had to deliver from 90 to 100 babies before she could take her final. The chief and sometimes his assistant drilled us in the skeleton, pelvis and fetus, and palpations to determine the positions of the fetus, as this was vital to the delivery process.

At the peak of our training, with the thought of having to do so many deliveries, many of us went out on the streets to find expectant mothers and brought them into the prenatal clinics. It was then that one had the chance to do all the necessary blood tests, urine analysis, blood pressure, vaginal examination, and palpations that we were taught. Whatever cases one brought in became one's patients. The mother and the nurse both got to know each other before the actual day of delivery came.

All findings were carefully recorded and filed away on all prenatal visits. The nurses were then placed on call a twenty-four-hour day, which meant that even when you were on night or day duties, sleeping or working or off duty, you were called as soon as your mother was admitted. The nurse on regular duty (chiefly during the night) would come to your room and knock on your door. "Nurse—, your mother, Mrs. H., is here. Come quickly, she is in labor."

During our waiting period, a nurse would go to bed half dressed, ready to act in five minutes and rush to the labor ward to examine and prepare for delivery and wait with her mother.

In those days no anesthesia was given during labor; the mother bore the pain, what we called the pain of joy, so here we'd go through the first, second, third pain of labor. "Bear down, Mother—hold your breath—don't push—now slowly the baby is coming—round, plump, smooth—the cord is cut—your baby is a boy!"

The baby was wrapped in a receiving blanket, shown to his mother, and put to rest in a bassinet in the adjoining room, while the nurse returned to wait with her mother for the final stage of labor. Thank God there were no complications and it was not necessary for the doctor to be called.

Your procedure was watched and supervised by the night or day supervisor. One hundred and eight of these cases were mine during nine intensive months of training. By the time of the terminal exams, I felt very confident and capable of handling any delivery. There were three days of theory and then one week went by before the scheduled date for the practical was posted.

We were in the large auditorium confronted by four obstetricians and gynecologists, two or three of them asking you the same question in a different way, sharp and to the point. Only one nurse entered this room at a time; an experience that no one looked forward to. We entered through one door and exited through a door on the other side of the room, making sure no one came in contact with the other nurses awaiting their test.

A couple of days after, I felt like a nervous wreck. A rumor was going around that some of the nurses had not made the grade. On meeting the chief M.D., I ventured to ask him how the exams went. He was always flying around in a long white coat and became known as "The Bird." Well, the bird took up speed on my question and replied while flying along, "I do not want to speak to any of you." That made me more sick; I was sick as a dog for a week. I could not say what was wrong, only I was sick and could not eat. I was referred to the nurse's physician. He could find nothing wrong. He said, "I cannot find anything the matter with you."

On returning from the physical examination, I met up with the assistant to the chief obstetrician. She called me into her office. "Sit down," she said. "What is the matter with you?" She spoke kindly to me and said, "Don't you worry about anything, you did not fail your exam." I stared at her amazed. She continued, "Yes, some failed, but you got the highest mark in the group."

I replied, "Are you sure? It is impossible for I was drilled with more confusing questions than anyone could imagine."

We sat in her office a while and discussed the ordeal of the oral examination and I told her how I was snubbed by the chief. Having spoken to someone who understood, I breathed a sigh of relief and all symptoms of my sickness disappeared.

Whatever I was told was confidential; it was sometime after, before the results were posted, that the girls came rushing to give me the news. There was elation all around for those who made it, and a taste of sadness for those who did not and had to sit the exams after six months more training.

All graduate nurses were required to spend the next three months practicing midwifery on the staff of the hospital, at which time we were given a certificate of proficiency, followed by a license of practice. Before the third month was completed, a call came for volunteers. It was the beginning of the Second World War and refugees were being housed in the military camp. I joined the volunteers and worked in the Evacuee Center that accommodated thousands of people fleeing their native land, seeking shelter on faraway shores to escape the ravages of war. The camp huts were turned into dormitories for the unfortunate. The greater part of the operation was governed and run by Roman Catholic nuns and priests.

The filth, dirt, and unsanitary conditions, and neglect were evident. One encountered cases of malnutrition, maggots, lice, and other parasites infecting most of the people we attended. Day after day we traveled some six or more miles to and from duty, as space was limited. Again, shoulder to shoulder, I found myself working among nuns. Some nuns were in charge of these dormitories.

One morning soon after starting, when I discovered an evacuee with lice and maggot infestation, I immediately reported to the doctor, further stating that I thought it was due to neglect of personal hygiene. The doctor spoke with the nun, the nun took her case to the priest, and again I had my second confrontation with a priest. He said I had insulted or abused or undermined the work being done by the good nuns. I knew it was not really true, so I responded that the good nuns had more to do than they could cope with, but the fact remained it was a case of neglect, not excluding the patient's responsibility. But the poor patient who could not communicate his needs in English and could not find free access to a bathroom was the one who suffered. I worked under these conditions with these people, doing more than I ever thought I could, but when the time was up, the camp was cleaner and more acceptable for living human beings and more satisfying. I parted friends with the priest and nuns.

I experienced a period of inactivity. I had labored to achieve for four years, during which time I occupied myself at home visiting my older relatives and resuming horseback riding, which I had not done for years. This I found to be most difficult, as the first time I got out I was full of pains the day after.

I went with my friend, who was then captain of the cricket team, to cricket matches some thirty miles from home when they were competing with the team in the next county. The cricket field was surrounded by huge shade trees, and the fife, guitar, and drums were the background music; lemonade, patties, stripe candies, bulla and coconut cakes were sold by vendors on the field. There was no stadium, so I sat in my friend's truck, and because the majority of the audience was men, I kept myself away from the crowd. It was fun to watch the match and cheer when my friend's team scored a run. We went home in high spirits after they won.

Not long after I completed my maternity training, I accepted a position called Nurse Instructor Grade I for the School of Home Economics, a government girls' boarding school of the Technical Training Centers. The school maintained a small clinic, a first aid center that served the district and allowed for students who were interested to practice nursing. I was responsible for the health of the staff and students.

There was a nursery with two babies, a part of the practice of infant care for the nursing student. Home nursing classes, first aid training, and district visiting were my well-defined duties. One student was assigned to assist me in the clinic and one to the nursery. The nursery was located in a large room with two cots for the babies and a single bed for the nursing student.

The superintendent of the Training Center was a big fat lady who was always well dressed and who wore a light coat to hide her bulges. She must have been in her late forties, and very seldom walked from her residence to the center, but was chauffeured around even though she could drive. When she got out of the car or station wagon she used a cane. The car was hers, but the station wagon belonging to the center was used for marketing and business trips.

Little Marjorie was the first baby to be brought to the center. She was nine months old with a round face, large, bright brown eyes and curly hair. Of course, she was pampered and petted by everyone, student and staff alike. She was a lovable child, cared for with exceptional excellence. Her clothes were made by the students. At bath time, a class would gather round to observe the bath procedure. After two years, Marjorie was adopted by the superintendent, but still remained at the center to be cared for under my guidance by the students.

Then came Peter, a frail, malnourished, Indian boy. He was given up for dead by the superintendent twice in one day. She sent for me, "Hurry up, Peter is dying." I dropped everything and walked up the hill to the nursery, at which time the superintendent was watching me and saying how could I be walking so leisurely along when Peter is so sick? I responded that a good nurse never gets excited or puts herself in a position where she cannot perform her duties. I told her later had I run up the hill I would have had to sit down and rest before I could help poor Peter, who was not really dying, but sound asleep. Peter had thrush and diaper rash and had special care all the time. Whenever the doctor visited the school, Peter was always checked. A big world awaited Peter out there, as day by day you could see him react to good care. He was later adopted by the assistant superintendent.

On district visiting days once each week, the class would make notes of the homes' existing conditions and what work we could do to help the needy. We traveled sometimes under the broiling sun, sheltered by umbrellas, and walked three miles along bridle tracks and the stony road. Always prepared for the worst, the class would prepare a cooked meal under the direction of the domestic science teacher to take to one old lady who lived in a dirt floor house with thatched and wattled walls and roof. At most times we cooked outdoors with a black pot or pan. On special days we had the good fortune to be chauffeured in the school's station wagon. On days when the old lady had to be cared for, for instance, washing her feet or combing her hair, soap and other toilet articles were taken along. All our efforts were put into the work of helping the needy. The entire staff stood behind us in this endeavor.

Persons who were seen and suspected to be sick were advised to go to the doctor, and those whom we could help came to the clinic to have their sores dressed, bandages applied, slings adjusted, compresses or poultices put on—all of which the student had to be well able to do before her final. Some of the students graduated with baby nursing certificates and some went on to the hospital to be trained as nurses. One I know went on to be a doctor after she finished.

During this time I applied for a study leave, as I was accepted by the Mothercraft Training Center to start extended training in Child Welfare work and Child Dietetics. The application was being processed for consideration at the next meeting of the Board. I felt after three years it was important for me to further my studies and take a study vacation abroad. At Cromwell House they specialized in Mothercraft, the care of the child from ages one to six. Just as I was waiting for the decision of the Board, my father succumbed to a massive heart attack.

The telegram reached me at 2 a.m.; a man was pounding on the door next to the sleeping quarters of the staff. I slept next to the physical or gym instructor; it was she who went to the door and brought me the telegram and accompanied me to the superintendent's quarters to awaken her and tell her the news. I never knew she was so softhearted, compassionate, and goodwilled until then. She immediately sent a message to the chauffeur and she gave me the use of her car.

The school was not less than two hundred miles away from my parents' home. Imagine yourself riding in the wee hours of the morning on rugged country roads with a few pieces of necessary clothing. I sobbed as we traveled on, feeling secure with the capable driver. It was not the driver; it was the car. World War II had just ended. Tires were rationed and petrol was scarce; the tires blew out three times during the trip, and consequently our progress was slow and frustrating.

Since it was my last duty to my father, I wired home to tell them that I would collect the casket from his nephew, who operated a funeral home one hundred and twenty miles away. The casket was tied to the top of the car and we journeyed on. We reached home just in time to meet the two clergymen coming in, and a crowd of relatives and friends waiting for the casket. With my head as big as a drum, we delivered the casket and without much fuss, the procession left for the church on the hill in which my parents were married thirty-six years before.

Pa was buried in the churchyard near the entrance gate, and sadness prevailed. For a long time none of us had experienced illness in the family, much less a sudden death.

The chauffeur returned the next morning, and I remained with Ma and the rest of the family for the ten days the government gave in emergency cases. The death of my father made me forget all my plans for studies abroad; this was deferred for one year. Of course, when I returned there was more work backlogged than I could get done and books to be corrected and upgraded for the coming exams. I worked full-time until late at night, but actually this was good for me.

Another year went by before I communicated with Cromwell House, and while a vacancy existed, they informed me I should be there to start the fall term. The Education Department (the branch of the government which supported the school) refused to grant me study leave, and that being decided, I resigned my position as Nurse Instructor Grade I, and left after the summer vacation.

It was a rush for me to go from one place to the other for a smallpox vaccination, TB tests, a complete physical, and then my passport. I left my home to go directly to the S.S. *Ariguana*, a large battleship that was used by the English in World War II and converted into a passenger vessel to start the four-thousand-mile voyage. Three of us young ladies occupied one cabin. It was a toss up as to who would sleep on the upper berth; the lot fell to me, but I made an exchange with the shorter and smaller girl.

All went well for the first few days; we were good company for each other and we skipped up and down the decks and played shuffleboard, until the other two girls began to throw up all they had eaten for breakfast. We still kept together as though we had known each other for years. We were a special group, young and full of all it took to enjoy life onboard the ship. We sat near the captain and chief officer's table.

I would get up early and do my exercises on the upper deck. It was there that I met the captain face to face, and he asked what I was doing up so early in the morning. I enjoyed talking with him, finding out something about England, London, and the places I was going to. Actually, I became a member of the crew since I was never seasick. I was asked to play the organ for Sunday services. We were in mid ocean, experiencing rough, high waves that made many passengers sick, and were consequently three days overdue. I remember the steward coming to ask me if I would help with some of the seasick.

A shout of joy was heard when the boat pulled in to Southampton. Jean and I parted good friends; all at once I was paged over the microphone by an escort of the British consulate, who was there to meet me, an overseas student. She met me onboard the ship, helped me through customs and immigration, and accompanied me to the hostel where the reservation was made for me to stay until the training session began. It was a large hostel for international students near South Kensington, near the Olympic games field and the famous Earl's Court. There could be found the renowned Harrod's, one of London's famed department stores, and also nearby were Selfridge's, Trafalgar Square, and Piccadilly Circus. All in all, an interesting location in southwest London. Most of the guests were students. The chaplain for overseas students visited me and invited me to the rectory, where I went on my free days.

A few days after my arrival, I was called by the hostess and told that Mothercraft Training Center had been in touch with her and requested that I go to the Oxford Street Uniform Center to get measured for my uniforms. Arrangements were made for an escort to take me there, and I was to be ready to leave after breakfast next morning. I prepared myself and we left early after breakfast. We hopped on a double-decker bus, the likes of which I had never seen before. I was not scared and I asked my escort if we could sit upstairs where I could get a good view of whatever we passed. I was all wrapped up in the scenery when the escort called out that we were to get out at the next stop. We moved slowly down; when the bus stopped, I jumped off. When I looked back, my escort was still on the bus. Glory be! Poor me, what was I to do? I checked my handbag and found I had two important things: the address of where I had to go, the uniform shop, and enough traveler's checks to pay for a taxi. I hailed the next taxi and went on my way.

When I arrived there, I announced myself and my purpose for being there. The lady said, "Oh, you are the one who got lost; you must not do that again. The hostel manager called and left a message for you to take a taxi back to the hostel when you are finished here. They also said you should get in touch with them right away, as you were given up for lost and missing." I telephoned right away and assured them I was all right and would be back before long. I got measured and thanked them graciously, went out and took a taxi to the hostel, where my escort met me still perplexed. "You see," she said, "when I said the next stop, I really meant the stop after this one." I told her I still did not understand her. The following week I went alone to Oxford Street to collect my uniforms.

Not many days went by and I took up residence in Cromwell House, Highgate Hill, about three miles away from Hampstead Heath. That is where you look down on the City of London. At Cromwell House I was met by Miss Maslen Jones, the director, who saw me as a youth not capable of traveling four thousand miles by myself. There were students at Cromwell House from Australia, New Zealand, Pakistan, Scotland, Ireland, and then there was I, from the British West Indies.

I can remember that it was late autumn, but I was prepared for the change of climate. My mother had made me long flannel nightgowns and a supply of warm underwear. I had settled in and managed to run across from the nurse's quarters to the nursery with my cap and uniform, just as the others. It seemed to me that all the other girls were used to the cold, wind and snow, and they wanted me to like it, too.

Since it was just after the war, one of my first duties was to work with a Scottish girl to clean out and prepare a room that was needed for the babies. Wearing masks, we took down unwanted items that were stored in the cots and bassinets, while some others took pictures of our activities. It took us two days.

My Australian friend taught me to cope. She would come to my room and watch me, and help me get settled. As time went on we did our studies and homework together and planned to shop on our days off. We got packages from home; she got butter from Australia, and I got sugar and homemade cakes. We shared our batch with our fellow nurses and reserved our special packages for each other. It was just after the war and these commodities were rationed. We found it hard to get by on our allotment.

Snowfall came early in November that year; such stuff I had never seen before. When there was enough on the ground, the English girls grew wild with excitement; they wanted to show the overseas students the beauty of Hampstead Heath and the magnificent view of the city below. My friend saw to it that I was properly dressed for the occasion: fleece-lined shoes, double-lined winter overcoat, and earmuffs. I did not know myself after I got dressed. With all the fuss and trouble of getting dressed, I did not make it. Six of us had started off. I had not gone more than a half mile up the winding, hilly road, when I started to feel numb.

The girls took turns holding me and dragging me along, saying, "Come on, you will get warmer as you go along." My feet became sticks under me and I began to cry. At this stage, Helen came to my aid and decided to go back with me.

It was a good thing I had proof rum (which I brought from home). My Australian friend used it to rub me down and gave me some of it in hot tea. Tears ran down my cheeks; I cried hysterically for about a half an hour. I still could not get warm. I lay there trembling; I really had been frostbitten. I missed class for a few days and felt sick as a dog. After that was over, it was fun again attending class and practicing good child care from birth. The babies came to us after they left the hospital. The mothers were kept in the hospital for nine days after delivery.

The diet of the child was supervised by the matron; the sterilization of the utensils was a special assignment that each student nurse had to do. Then there was a special bathroom preparation and the care of the nursery.

As in all nursing fields there was day and night duty and the twelve-hour shift. We experimented with the babies. Some were put on the balcony, an unheated room with open screened windows. The babies were wrapped snugly in flannel and wool blankets. These babies slept from 10 p.m. until they were awakened and made ready for the 6 a.m. feed.

All six months of training ended with rigorous examinations.

The New Zealand girls I met went their own ways, so did the Indian girls, but my Australian friend stayed with me. We always had things in common. Her boyfriend was a midshipman who worked between Australia and England, and she was busy doing her trousseau. So when he ran off and married another girl, my friend offered me her trousseau. I refused because I felt that she was too sweet a girl, and someday she would meet the right man, and I encouraged her to keep it.

After all my batch mates left, I was sent for by the nursing director. When I went into her office she presented me with an application form (as a matter of fact) and asked me to remain on staff and assist in training of the child care baby nurses. This I did for seven months, and left Highgate Hill to reside in southwest London to start post-graduate studies in cancer and allied diseases. The hospital was called the Royal Cancer Hospital, on Fulham Road, near Earl's Court, just behind the international hostel where I spent my first four weeks in England.

The matron and charge nurse were very friendly. All the nurses were exposed to radiation and were given radiosensitive discs to wear, which were checked every two weeks for the extent of x-ray contact, along with a monthly blood count. Everything was extremely different, from the nursing of the babies onward, but once you got started, it was all easy routine. There was no emergency room in this hospital. Patients were referred to this hospital and admitted to the ward where we would take all routine blood tests.

By the way, the hospital was called "Royal" because of its association with the royal family. I remember well my encounter with Sir Thomas Price who was then the physician for King George VI. For he, like most of the English people I had met, had not seen anyone like me before, who spoke English with such a distinct accent, and inquired where I was from. His patient, an Englishman, was one of the proudest men on the floor because he had the same physician as the king. Never did he mind how sick he was; he was given six months to live and had gone a year over the six months. He could not understand how anyone could make such a great mistake.

My Australian friend visited me for tea, and we laughed and cried together as she took off for home. I was brokenhearted at Christmas and was sad even when on duty. That is when the charge nurse said, "Cheer up, we'll soon be dead. How can you, a big girl, miss your home?"

She was a tough English girl who had served in the army and, I found out later, she had no real family life. Before I finished my year in training, the charge nurse resigned and went to be a waitress in the Lyon's Corner House.

One day I was sent to the laboratory to collect blood. While walking along the long corridor, I stumbled with the crate of blood. I bruised my knee to save four pints of blood, just a stroke of luck. I was sometimes left in charge of the ward after the charge nurse resigned.

The large sterilization unit off the ward could tell many a story. It was here gossip and flirting went on, and it was where I developed my septic finger, and then I learned that each resident in the U.K. had to be registered with a doctor in whichever district one lived. I registered with a general doctor that evening, and under local anesthesia I had my fingernail removed, and obtained sick leave for three days.

When I resumed work I was relieved from actual nursing care and did much of the desk work, picking up physicians' orders, writing reports, and checking to see that all orders were carried out. When I got the responsibility of charge nurse, it was a test for me to show the doctor or matron that I was capable of handling all related duties.

When the time came for me to leave England, the doctor asked that I stay and offered me a permanent position. I do not know what she found in me, but it made me feel good when she said, "You have been a tower of strength to all of us."

I decided to go to northwest London to visit a friend who was a medical student at the University of London. I traveled underground by tube; it was another experience for me. An Englishman who kept staring at me changed trains with me. He traveled up the elevator with me while my heart kept pounding. I wondered what was next. As soon as the elevator landed, I ran across the street and jumped into a taxi. I felt that the taxi saved me from whatever he was up to.

When I got to my friend's apartment I was still frightened, but he told me that happened in London every day. After supper I took a taxi back home; I was too scared to go on the train.

The chaplain for overseas students invited me to tea at his residence. He was a Scotsman, and heard his wife told me all I wanted to know about Scotland and advised me to visit Scotland before returning home.

After, I had tea with my English nursing instructor, who spent her better days as matron in the West Indies and played a great part in my training, I booked a trip to France and later to Scotland and Wales. We crossed the English Channel and landed in Le Havre. We took a taxi to the hotel a few blocks away from the Arch of Triumph, joined a town party on a bus to Versailles, spent about two hours going through Louis XV's Palace, then on return, the party stopped for a short time for us to view the Eiffel Tower and back.

After a tiring but interesting day, I accepted the luxury of ringing for breakfast in bed next morning, and was ready to walk to the Arch and Notre Dame and do some shopping. It was fun walking around Paris, only knowing a few words of French. But people were helpful, and I had a translation dictionary. I took in one night at a club, but left before it was too late. After four days in Paris, I returned to my room in London to take off again for Scotland.

I started off alone. The bus was a comfortable sleeper coach. We left London just before sunset and I think the route was one of the most scenic I have seen up through Manchester, to Liverpool, and to Edinburgh.

Reservations were made for me to spend my five days in Edinburgh with a Scottish family. The couple was middle-aged and very courteous and friendly. We were not far from the Palace and the Castle. When I told them I would like to see the Royal Mile, they replied that the only way I would get to see that was to walk. The Royal Mile is the distance of a mile between the Palace and the Castle. The pavement was good to walk on, but it was uphill.

After shopping around Edinburgh and viewing the rugged hills, I returned to London to take off again for a weekend in Wales. I went to the Cardiff Castle and the Friars Botanical Gardens. I got back to London in time to visit the American Embassy and apply for a visa to travel via the U.S. I saw all the cathedrals, Windsor Castle, Buckingham Palace, Hampton Court, Tower Bridge, and Covent Garden. I went to the Royal Albert Hall, Trafalgar Square, Piccadilly Circus, St. James Park and saw all the main attractions, such as the changing of the guard.

When King George VI died, I was on night duty, but we were given a special permit to go early and enter through the door reserved for royalty so as not to have a long wait. We went in full uniform with our red and blue caps and were hurried past the casket in Westminster Abbey. The proclamation of Queen Elizabeth II was carried out on the balcony of Buckingham Palace the same evening that her father died, and I was among the thousands of viewers.

I was on a merry-go-round those days. The last week I spent in England I had some of the most enjoyable days of my life. It was there I met Joe the aircraft machinist, Jim the druggist, and Sam the park manager. Joe became my husband; we got married in a simple ceremony in Ealing, Middlesex, England, with my sister as maid of honor and Jim as the best man. We settled down in Greenford, Middlesex, a suburb of London.

In St. James Park during the late spring, one could not help but be impressed by the beauty of the landscape—the tulips in full bloom. I returned several times just to see the changing of the guard and the trouping of the colors. I worshiped at Westminster Abbey and St. Paul's Cathedral.

I returned to Roosevelt Square, picked up my visa, changed my sterling currency into dollars, and made reservations on the B.O.A.C. Airlines, well spent. I picked up my belongings, including gifts for my mother and the rest of my family; everyone got a little souvenir of the British Isles and France. The flight was uneventful until the disembarkment through immigration. There was a thorough check and inquiry as to how long I intended to remain in the U.S., then on to customs. But since the final destination was not the U.S., I was treated as an in transit visitor. My sister met me and I stayed with her for a month until I was ready to take off again.

Actually, before I left London, I was advised by the matron of the Royal Cancer Hospital to get in touch with the State Department in Albany if I had any intention of practicing nursing in the U.S. That was not my problem at the time. I thought New York City was too hectic and the pace was too fast for me; the stores were too crowded, I got pushed aside to board the bus or subway, and inside the stores, it was no different. After coming from a city like London, I found it to be a rather drastic contrast.

I had my invitation and left for my home in the West Indies. After I told my mother and others about my experiences and travel, I started to settle down and get ready for my return to the U.S. Since I was given a permanent visa in London, I had no difficulty in returning.

Not long after I got back, I received a letter from Albany that I had to sit for their State Board Exams. They did not accept my qualifications and experience in the nursing field, until I submitted all dates, directors, hospitals, and testimonial certificates, license, school of nursing, country and address, before I qualified for an Associate's degree.

While I waited for the state exams and the results thereof, I was given a temporary license. On obtaining the permanent state license, I was further advised that unless there was proof of my U.S. citizenship, my license would be revoked. I did private duty nursing and worked as a relief nurse.

After getting myself established, I returned to England. This time I flew in a plane with a defective engine and we came down in Preswick, Scotland. As the pilot stated, "Had we gone straight to London we would never see each other again." All passengers eyed each other and I blessed myself and prayed. The plane was delayed four long hours. All this time Joe waited for me at the London airport. There was lots of excitement as I rushed through customs again. We took a taxi home. It was almost autumn and I started to forget how to keep warm.

We settled in Greenford, Middlesex, a suburb approximately forty miles southwest of London. We lived in a two-story flat with two large bedrooms and a bathroom upstairs, and a dining room, living room, entrance hall, and kitchen downstairs. Past the kitchen was the conservatory and a large lot with apple, peach, and plum trees, and in front was a small plot for flowering plants, surrounded by a picket fence that added some privacy from Hurley Road and the adjoining neighbors.

The winter was damp and cold. With convector gas heat, each room had its own fireplace. We burned coal in the dining room. Joe would have coal delivered to keep the room warm. I guess it was the stove in the kitchen that kept us warm. Each room had a different temperature.

The Scottish nurse, Janet, married to a squadron leader in the R.A.F. who was now a professor of aviation at the University of London, called on me to help her take care of an old lady who lived with her. It was then I started to get those awful chilblains and had to go to the doctor, who advised me to return to the U.S.

Pinky came to tea a few times, also Jean, the girl I traveled with on my first voyage. When spring came and the weather was dry, it was Frank and Janet who went with us on a picnic to the cliffs of Dover.

The days went by and Joe and I decided that I could return to the U.S. It was not the nicest thing to happen, but I could not face the damp cold. Joe planned to pull up sticks and join me as soon as I found a place and was settled in the U.S. This time accompanied by Joe and Pinky, I journeyed from Middlesex to Southampton for my voyage back to the U.S. We were six days at sea on the S.S. *U.S.A.* My sister met me at Pier Four. I think it was good to set my feet on solid ground, even though I enjoyed the voyage.

It was late spring and the weather was just right. I lived with my sister for a few weeks. In those days new buildings were going up all over New York City. I got a brand new three-and-a-half-room apartment that was just right for Joe and me. After signing a three-year lease and paying $700 for the first month's rent and one month's security, I moved in with all new furniture. We were then paying for an elevator and doorman's service.

Joe came in early summer and before long he decided we should look for another place that was less expensive. Again we got a new apartment, about two miles away from where we stayed, for $100 less. No doorman, but it was a pretty neat and secure place.

I was selected as a visiting nurse and was assigned to Brownsville. I started out frightened because I heard people got killed like flies in this area. Strange as it seems, I was content to carry on. What bothered me most was finding the streets and numbers of the buildings in the housing projects. On one occasion, after getting lost, I was so tired out that when I got to the apartment, after conveying the patient to a wheelchair, I stumbled over and landed in bed.

Nine months later, I resigned and accepted a position as nurse supervisor assistant to the director of the Hebrew Home and Hospital. It was a position in which I worked for two years and then took on another supervisor post in a nursing home. Strangely enough, I had less responsibility and a substantial increase in salary. This new assignment allowed me more time at home.

We were now encouraged to buy and obtain a co-op duplex that we called home for four years. It was in a new section, a private housing development facing the beach, where we could see the large ships go by not far from the Verrazano Narrows Bridge.

The two bedrooms and bath upstairs had a balcony, and the dining and living room combined downstairs with the kitchen and powder room. In all, there were five closets to store belongings. We also had a garden plot in front that we made into an attractive flower garden. This is where we met Renata, Tony, and their two daughters, Monica and Cora. We shared love at Christmas and Thanksgiving. One year we had them for Thanksgiving and they had us for Christmas. It was a busy, enjoyable time in our lives.

Time went by and I did my supervisor duties in the nursing home, and helped in the rehabilitation unit of the city hospital for four hours each day, then rushed home to make supper. Although there were times when I had supper ready that was half prepared the day before, many times there was no time to make supper at all.

One vacation we were planning to go on a Caribbean cruise. My husband helped me to decide, and I resigned both positions with the view of having my freedom to do whatever I wanted when I returned.

We planned to purchase a home with quarters large enough for us to live in and use the remaining space for a rest home. We looked at houses in Brooklyn, and actually we were on our way to look at one in the Saranac Lakes area, when we were directed to look at one in Otsego County, where nothing was yet settled. I submitted my resignation and was told by the administrator that he refused to accept it, and expected me to return after the vacation period. Already, plans were made for the cruise and we discovered that my husband's leave was not granted. I kept my reservation and canceled his and agreed for him to fly down one week later.

During this time I went to the State Department to tell them of my intentions of going into business, and requested that the property in which I was interested be inspected to determine whether it was suitable. That being done, I left on the cruise to Puerto Rico, the Virgin Islands, St. Thomas, St. Kitts, and Curaçao. We had a day or two in each port to visit points of interest and return to the ship for the night. Our last port southward was to be Jamaica, where I took leave of the cruise, was met by my sister at Kingston Harbor, and left for home the next day.

After a few days, Joe flew down and we met him at the Montego Bay airport. Since he had not seen the island before, we drove slowly through the beautiful hills of St. James on to the scenic bamboo groves in Lacovia and on along the Santa Cruz Mountains home. Going from Mother's home to spend some time with my brother in Malvern, we went on to Pedro Plains and Black River. On the whole, we had a wonderful vacation.

After two weeks in Jamaica, we flew back to New York. There was news waiting for me from the State Department. It was necessary that more visits be made to the department to make out a formal application for going into rest home activities. The home was purchased, and negotiations continued. Several visits were made by the inspectors, and additional alterations were made and a license obtained from the department. It was a relief to know we could now sell our duplex and settle down to live quietly and be occupied with our own business. I returned to the duplex, packed as much as I could, and moved the lighter stuff.

On moving day we had a snowstorm. I traveled down, doing ten, maybe twenty miles per hour. When I stopped in the rest area, a man saw me cleaning the windshield and said, "You shouldn't bother, there is more to come, you're wasting your time."

Lo and behold, when I reached New York City the moving man did not show up. My husband called to find out why. The reply was, "Didn't you know we had a snowstorm upstate?" That made me stay one day longer.

Joe, who had planned to retire, decided to go on working and rented an apartment in Brooklyn. It was his choice. When I got back to the new home, the first gentleman was ready to take up residence. From that time on I lost my freedom. I felt my first responsibility was the comfort of my guests.

The people of the community showed much apprehension at my presence and would ask questions such as, "How did you get up here?" Many of them stated that they wanted to purchase the home but could not afford it. The old house was built in 1906 by the first president of the bank and made history for the town. Life went on, and business progressed slowly. I was well established in business and lived comfortably there.

My oldest longtime friend had promised to spend some time with me. Then suddenly she decided to come up for a two-week stay. I met her, her husband, and her brother at the Greyhound bus terminal and brought them home. We settled in, ate a nice dinner, chatted and listened to old records, then retired to bed.

Not long after retiring, the doorbell rang and a messenger presented a telegram announcing my mother's progressive decline. I still cannot remember what happened or how I arranged everything, but I took off.

Half Sleeping, Half Waking
The Story of My Mother's Death

I lay there in bed,
Eyes closed, thinking.
Suddenly a pair of hands
Suspended in midair above.
My mother's hands, behold!
Clean, smooth and childlike!
A feeling of awe came over me.
My mother, ninety-six.

How could it be? I could not sleep!
Then a voice called.
The doorbell rang, "a cable"
Bearing tidings of a mother.
Her days were coming to a close,
Must I sit or go?

Awake, half asleep
Midnight came, anxiously I hurried.

A Nurse's Journey

Could I drive?
Call a travel agent,
I must be quick. I have to go.
My friend will you go with me
To the road through the mountains
Down the lane to the trail
To catch the plane?
The clouds are low,
The stars are dim,
Help me, my God,
I have to go.
The speed to go ... the radar,
Limitations, I have to fly.
The town, the cities,
The roads are blocked.
The beat of my heart,
My pulse confuses me,
Those hands I see.

Push some clothes,
Anything, into a bag.
To the highway, the streets,

The hills, they fly before my eyes,
Rolling on and on I go,
Low then high.
Two thousand miles away to
Those hands stretched out before her,
Like a child clasping for something
She cannot reach.
Pray for me, stay with me,
I heard her say.
My mother waking, then asleep,
Her hand still by her side.

My youngest sister made reservations on B.O.A.C., flight 707, and away we went. The delay at the airport seemed longer than I could take. I had an open ticket because of the nature and purpose of my journey. Well, the customs officer (who must have had a fight with someone before he got me) gave me ten days to leave the country. "My, my," I said to myself, "who knows what will happen?"

My other sister and a chauffeur were waiting to meet us. Through the winding, hilly roads we journeyed, through magnificent mountains; the tropical sun and sea coast setting would almost make one forget one's troubles. We got to my brother's home on the steep hill where my mother had lived for the past year. Since she was getting feeble, we all agreed that although she had a live-in maid, she should not be left all alone. The old lady was ninety-six years old, conscious and still able to sit up for short intervals.

The doctor came to see her the following day and gave us the news; it was only a matter of time. All five of us met there and remained together until Mammy died five days later. I remember her labored breathing when I left to go to the next room to take a nap. Soon after, my sister called to say, "Come, Mammy is not breathing."

We all huddled together for a while. I did the necessary care and contacted the doctor, the minister and the undertaker. We buried our mother in the churchyard, the burial ground where my father was buried some twenty-three years before. The heavens opened to receive her. For never had I seen such large raindrops before, and so our mother left us.

On the tenth day, I left the island for the U.S. Two years after I started the business, my husband at last decided to retire. It was business as usual, government inspectors were coming around every three to six months. We had parties at Christmastime for the guests and their relatives. The large family room had the fireplace aglow, and with homemade cookies and cakes, party crackers and funny hats, and Christmas carols sung by all, who said it wasn't fun?

Often we would have a picnic under the trees in the back with the Hibachi and glowing coals, some of the happy summer days. Other times we packed lunches and motored to the public parks and sat on the benches with the birds and squirrels around. All these activities were enjoyed by the residents and employees alike, and for me it was fun planning and great satisfaction watching and partaking.

Shortly after retiring, my husband returned to Ireland to visit his relatives. He was always busy doing everything he could find to do. I often watched him cutting four by fours to put up a partition to make an extra room in the basement.

One Saturday he said, "I am going shopping." It could not have been more than three hours later when the telephone rang. A voice at the other end said, "This is to let you know that your husband is a patient in the hospital," and continued explaining that he went to the emergency room for treatment and was admitted. Everything comes to me in surprises. I never knew my husband was sick; he never told me he was not feeling well. I hurried and called my friend who drove me to the hospital after I had gotten all his necessary clothing together.

Hazel McShane

When I arrived at the hospital, I found that no doctor had yet seen him, only the house doctor. The outlook was not good; he was being given oxygen. The next day, Joe called and said that the doctor was making up his mind to do surgery. He said, "I am frightened to death! Come and take me out of this place."

When I got there, he told me the anesthesiologist told him that many of these types of patients die on the operating room table. I assured him that no one could operate without his signing a consent. I would call a thoracic surgeon with whom I had worked and explain everything to him when I got home. I was lucky enough, and a date was set for consultation. The next day I went to the hospital, signed him out, got all his records straight and we left for home.

I cried and fretted as I knew that my husband's breathing was not good. I packed his case with everything I could think of for the hospital, and the next morning we left for the long ride on the bus and taxi to the consultant's office. The doctor was all ready for us, gave Joe a thorough examination and admitted him into the hospital. The surgeon told me that, had they operated on him, he surely would have died. He was kept in the hospital and treated for two full weeks of intensive treatment in preparation for surgery. After returning home and putting my business in order, and getting one of my dependable assistants to stay in for me, I returned to the city to be with Joe after surgery.

The doctors and nurses were great. The doctor told me the growth on the left lobe of his lung was almost the size of an orange and was malignant in nature. This was confirmed by the test afterwards. Can you imagine living with this and keeping it a secret from Joe? The doctor told him that, had it not been removed, it would have become cancerous. Recovery from the surgery went well; then came time for discharge. I returned with the car to take him home, but he was too weak to travel, so I left him with my sister in the city until the doctor gave him the OK to take the journey. With Joe propped up on three pillows, I took off from New York City, took a detour over the George Washington Bridge, and landed us in New Jersey. It was slow going all the way, stopping at all parking exits and service stops, taking almost four hours to get home.

Business in the home picked up, my hands were more than full while I took full charge of my husband's bed, bath, meals, and medication. I was fortunate to have a competent helper who was a capable and reliable assistant, Babs. She was sweet and attentive to everyone. I depended on her and she never let me down. Slowly Joe started to regain his strength and walk around and occupy himself without much strain.

The Department of Licensing now demanded changes in the building. Smoke detectors and fire alarm systems were to be installed. No one in this town or nearby had such equipment available. I made several inquiries and got a manufacturer in Massachusetts to supply all that was required, and so the local electrician did the contract to get the work done. Before long, there were two false alarms that the manufacturers had to check before the unit was declared safe for use.

So life went on and Joe had to visit the surgeon in New York who was pleased with his progress and referred him to the local doctor. His condition changed for the better and Joe was almost on his own again. His brother and sister-in-law came over to visit him. He was well enough to go with me to meet them at Kennedy Airport. The plane did not get in until late that evening so we stayed at a Howard Johnson Motel in Spring Valley. We took a double room; Joe and I in one bed, and Pat and Maureen in the other, and we spent the night there and had breakfast the next morning before continuing the 120 mile journey. It was a pleasant morning.

The day was warm, a moderately nice day, and we enjoyed the drive up through the Catskills. The three weeks in Worcester went well for the visitors. We took them to all the points of interest and even dined in the famous and exclusive Otesaga Hotel. Back home to celebrate, we all planted the border of shrubs in back of the plot.

We went back to New York, visited with my sisters and went on to Queens, where we dined at the Knights' home. I cannot forget how Pat made the old piano sing with his rich melodies. We visited the Empire State Building, shopped on Fifth Avenue, and went on to Macy's. They left the next day by Aer Lingus, back to green Ireland. We had telephone conversations with them shortly after they reached Ireland.

Just one week passed when Joe walked down to the post office three blocks from home. He returned with a cablegram and an airmail letter. Joe handed me the letter and he opened the telegram. His countenance changed and he appeared faint. Pat had died.

"Oh, no," I said, "Let me see." We cried together. It was as though Pat had come all this way to say good-bye to his only brother. Joe instantly decided he had to go to the funeral. Again I went packing, putting together all I thought necessary for him to take. Concerned about him taking such a long trip after his major surgery, I called the surgeon. "What! If he feels that good and wants to go, let us not stop him. But I feel he is a brave man to be going." We talked most of that night.

Next morning I drove him to the Greyhound bus stop. He went as we both told each other to take care. As soon as I got home, I telephoned Ireland, giving them the flight number and expected time of arrival and asking them to take care and see that Joe did not make himself a pallbearer since the funeral was delayed until he arrived. Well, he got to Belfast later, and no one could stop him. I was told that he was doing just what he wanted to—bearing the casket. After the burial, he became sick in Ireland and sought the advice and treatment of the doctor over there. He left Ireland worse than he had left here. The same night he returned to the U.S., I called the doctor in New York and the next day he was admitted into the hospital. He was now skin and bones and could barely speak. On coming home, he had to visit the local doctor every so often. No one knew the pains I suffered watching my husband just wasting away.

He was referred to a radiologist who recommended chemotherapy. The surgeon was not in agreement, saying that radiation of this kind would do him no good in the end. However, he started back and forth, two times a week, thirty-two miles each way, to have treatment for nine weeks. He suffered the usual progressive loss of appetite from the treatment; he could only take beef tea, homemade from pure lean steaks with no fat, and custards or clear liquids. Overnight, when I thought he had taken all he could take, he vomited everything and with the bathroom nearby, it was easy for me to care for him.

Gradually his breathing became difficult, the radiologist came out at midnight, brought emergency oxygen and ordered a standby set, which was set up so Joe could give it to himself, but most times he would call for me. I remembered to ask him if he wanted the priest, although I know he had already been given the "last rites" of the Roman Catholic church. So I called the priest of the nearby town. By the next week he was showing signs of improvement and could walk around again. We said the Novena of St. Martin's together every day before lunch.

He took all his medication and vitamins and had to be given oxygen quite frequently. I got a hospital bed that he rejected. I could not stand to see him suffering and losing ground day after day. I stayed by him night after night to help him bear the pain (if such is possible) and to comfort him.

After speaking with the doctor one morning he said, "Bring him in and let us suction him." We went with one of my aides who helped to put him in the car. I drove with him sitting beside me. There was such a long delay when we reached the hospital that by the time they got to him he was fit for admission. I had a strong feeling that I should take him back home, for I realized Joe was near death.

I visited the next day and brought with me a cup of his favorite beef tea. I fed him some and left the rest in the thermos. The last audible words he said to me I will not forget: "You should be here in the night to see what goes on."

Five days later, my sister came to visit me and we went together to see Joe. He did not speak a word. I took home all his clothes and waited for the news. That same night God and his angels came and took Joe home, away from all his pain.

Although I requested that they should not perform an autopsy, the doctor called again to get permission for one. It was Joe's request to be buried by the same priest who came that night to give him the last rites. His nephew from Ireland came over and we journeyed seventeen miles to Mount Calvary on the side of a hill where Joe was buried. By the way, it was early '76 and there was much snow on the ground.

Life went on dull and full of activities. It was Joe's request that his clothes be given to the Salvation Army. After a few days, I got boxes of clothes together and we drove some twenty miles away to deliver them. No one understood that the thought of facing the simple everyday tasks was harder for me. At this stage I decided to close the adult home, surrender my license and go away.

The following year all the relatives of my guests were sent a circular type of letter: "To whom it may concern, Mrs. McShane, proprietor of the home for adults in the town of Worcester, wishes to announce that she will not renew her operating license which expires in August. As of August 31, 1977, the home will no longer be in operation. Mrs. McShane wishes at this time to express her deep appreciation to all who have, by their cooperation or patronage, made the home a viable operation." One by one the residents left; only I remained.

Something was waiting for me, a message from the island requesting me to come down. I left the business in the hands of my most competent assistant, packed my clothing together and was away for five weeks. At this time, my brother had fallen on the floor of his bedroom, his favorite dog Dolly by his side. He had suffered a stroke; the doctor ordered him hospitalized. The nearest ambulance was four miles away, the only contact was the public telephone.

The doctor took care of this. When the ambulance came, it had one driver, one attendant, a stretcher, and no sheet, pillow or blanket. We supplied the necessary. With the patient secure, off it went with me holding the patient still while the ambulance traveled, bobbing up and down over the winding, steep hills and dusty roads. The trip took four hours, there was no delay, and there was no such thing as a private room in the hospital. He was put in a corner bed of a ward.

Can you imagine putting a stroke patient to bed with no side rails? The next thing I saw was the possibility of his falling out of bed. "Nurse," I said, "there are no side rails on the bed." She replied, "We have none, that is why we put him in the corner."

The doctor was kind, interested, and offered much consolation, but that would not do. Next day we visited brother, he had abrasions on his leg and face. Sure enough, he had fallen out of bed. This being the case, he was moved to the other corner. When it was time for me to return and close out my business, the remaining two guests were placed in facilities selected by their relatives.

Before long I found I had to return to the island to care for my brother. It was the decision of my sister and the doctor that he should be placed in a rehabilitation center some ninety miles from his home. Not being able to get ahold of the doctor, I called the nearby police station and left a message to tell the doctor the only place my brother is to go after discharge from the hospital is his home. My sisters were furious, they felt that I was not cooperating with the doctor. So he was discharged to his home and left in the care of a nervous sister who, not being a nurse, was scared of everything.

From flight 407 Pan Am, I got there and took over. An elderly lady, reported to be a good physiotherapist, came in twice a week and then once weekly to give him exercises. Do you want to hear what went on? "Now, come, come, you can pull my hand out like that. I am a sick man, my skin is like a baby, treat me tenderly." She quipped back, "Sickness drives car, come and walk, foot go away."

I got a wheelchair with a special permit sent down from the U.S. and had him taken to the nearest hospital for better rehabilitation, while I did the follow-up exercises with him at home. I had ramps put on the backstairs to the garage and indoors, too. The rushing to and fro went on for three months until the doctor and I felt my brother had enough therapy and should now continue at home. By this time he was gaining confidence and could walk with a walker. My brother was able to walk to the car, shed his shoes and help dress himself.

The day of saying good-bye was a sad and unforgettable one. Everybody started to cry and with the driver being late, I thought I would never reach the airport in time. I was on the verge of throwing up, giving the birds and the dogs all I had eaten that morning, and at the same time I was literally wetting my pants.

Passing through the bamboo grove as in a dream, the car flew to get there. We got to the airport just in time for me to be the last person rushing through immigration, then up the collapsing stairway leading to the plane. With me puffing and blowing like a train, the stewardess was saying, "What happened to you? We were just getting ready to take off."

I was so rushed I could scarcely answer except to say, "I am sorry I was late," that's all, such a thing had never happened to me before. When dinner was served I could not eat a thing. We reached Kennedy Airport, circled around a few times and ended with a smooth landing and much applause for the pilot. My youngest sister was there to meet me. Rushing through customs was now becoming a way of life for me and the old violin. I spent the night at my sister's talking over the happenings of the past months. A day after I took off again, I stopped overnight with another sister on Riverside Drive, talked all night and got up the next morning.

Now anxious to return home, I was dragging my suitcases around the hallway and through the double doors and shuffling down the sidewalk to where my car was parked. Then I jumped in and took off. It was just daybreak and very few cars were moving upstate. I made the trip in three and one half hours. It was the end of the first quarter and time to file my last year's income tax. That done, I was ready to go into retirement in this large empty house.

Suddenly something struck me and I started to think that after all, I could still be useful. I ventured to volunteer in the peace corps. I traveled on roads I never heard of before. I had my route mapped out by the AAA up to Elmira. I had interviews with officials to answer questions from birth through '77. I told them all I knew and took home forms to be filled out in relation to my life and achievements. I was a person ready and willing to serve other people not as fortunate as myself.

I went through all the preliminaries: fingerprints, medical x-rays, E.K.G., teeth, certification, blood tests, height, weight, stress test. With all the tests completed, I was sent forms with information for placement. The medical record was sent straight to Washington, and about two weeks later I was told I had failed the stress test and could not be given an overseas assignment. The same report recommended that I join VISTA, the national arm. This left me shocked beyond words.

No wonder I had failed the stress test, I had gone through so much these past four years. I was struck with disappointment and did not respond enthusiastically to the voice at the end of the line that said, "A good volunteer goes wherever she is sent." Thereupon, I gave in willingly.

Hazel McShane

I was put in touch with Supervision in Atlanta and told that an organization of Southern Cooperation was looking for a nurse for its medical center to start work immediately. Another message came through urgently, flight 305 booked on Delta Airlines, January 27, 1978, and I should pick up my ticket at LaGuardia and change planes at Atlanta and wait for Southern Belle to Tuscaloosa. I had never heard of such a place before. I then went to my sister's to say good-bye. My sister and brother-in-law took me to the airport and off I went to places unknown.

When we came down in Atlanta I started to feel at a loss. I roamed around for six hours before the Southern plane came. Through long winding ramps I shuffled to my seat in the plane for the short ride to Tuscaloosa. There I waited in a small dusty waiting room, not knowing who would meet me.

I claimed my baggage and then I saw two men, one was Mr. Brown, a young bearded man who introduced himself as the director of the medical center and inquired after me. The other, Mr. Palmer, was the custodian of the center. They led the way and took me to the car. "By the way," asked the custodian, "is this all your baggage? Did you sleep? So how was the flight down?"

"Good," I replied, "only the long stopover in Atlanta made me tired."

With the two suitcases safely in the trunk of the car and Mr. "P" sitting in the backseat, Mr. "B" at the wheel of the car sped off through long dusty roads in rural Atlanta. So this was the co-op. "The main office is here," said Mr. B. He politely opened the door. "Please come with me to meet our chief executive director of the co-op."

This gentleman too was bearded and rather distinguished as he rose from his seat and greeted me, expressing hopes that I'd like Epes and enjoy my stay with them. Then I was escorted to meet all the members of the co-op on duty. After this, I was brought to a place that really was a trailer camp. Mr. B said, "This is your trailer." As he opened the door I was hit by an odor. I wondered if it was the smell of dead rats and rotten fruits and vegetables with human excretion all mixed together and a dirty mattress on the floor. I turned back to the car. I begged to be taken back to the airport as it appeared that they were really not ready for anyone.

With this, the distinguished executive was called over. He offered his apologies: he thought that the trailer had been cleaned. The director of the medical center and the other gentleman decided that I should spend the night in the nearby motel. We rushed over to the medical center. I met all the employees and was shown all the rooms. From there I went to the motel to dine; the director paid the way, and I spent the night, leaving my larger case at the center.

I spent the night still dazed and stunned partly from the traveling and partly from the shock of the dirty trailer. I was only half dressed, for now I remembered that my nightclothes were in the case I had left behind several miles away. The next thing I did was find a public telephone to phone my sister and tell her all my experiences up to now.

The morning after, I think I was the first one in the breakfast room. The waiter said, "You are rather early, we do not serve breakfast before 8:00 a.m."

"Never mind," I said, "if you don't object, I will sit here until you are ready, for someone is coming to fetch me and I do not know what time he or she will arrive." The breakfast was simple: orange juice, coffee, and toast; that's all I could take.

Sure enough, an outreach worker whom I met at the medical center came for me at 8:00 a.m. I got a message to book in for one more night at the motel. In less than one hour, we arrived at the medical center. There had been a part-time nurse from the nearby hospital helping them out and, worse still, they had been operating for months without a doctor. So it was then that I took over.

The director came up with a suggestion that day that I stay with a retired lady in the district to share a trailer with an outreach volunteer who was from the area. It was then I started to see how I would have to live. For supper, the outreach worker made me pig's ears and black-eyed peas. I never before had such a combination, but I enjoyed it. Thereafter, I was picked up by a worker from the center since I had no car and there was no public transportation. When I got to the center that day, I met the secretary, a thin wiry lady who looked younger than she was and had four children of her own.

The State Education Department wanted proof of my New York State license. It was the secretary who took me to the little photo shop to have pictures taken and copies of my license. A few weeks later a permit to work at the center came through. It now became compulsory for all VISTA nationals and domestics to attend monthly meetings at the County Regional Supervision. It was there that I met Fred, a refined and educated architect who worked for the corps. He was married to a white woman and had three children. He decided to drive us to the meeting in Selma.

The county supervisor of the program, a rough mannered person who claimed to have given up teaching to take the job, was out of order altogether. He chewed tobacco and spat on the floor around the platform while addressing the audience. A good thing no one sat near or they would have been spat on. He swore and never spoke correctly, but I was told he spoke the language the local people liked to hear. It was a shocking experience for me. I went to the meetings called in-service training. Fred agreed with me saying, "To tell the truth, I detest the behavior of the man."

There were days I felt I must get away, but I had made my mind up to do the work so long as I was able. This was the Year of the Child, remember, the emphasis is on the child. Our motto for the center was C.C.C. (Community, Compassion, and Care). Community: dedicated to provide the best possible health care to the community. Compassion: a warm, interested attitude to all entrusted to our care. Care: the place where people really care.

The Center operated as a voluntary, nonprofit health center. Its services were offered in accordance with the Department of Health, Education and Welfare of the state. The outreach workers were the greatest link between the center and the community.

Children came from all around to be certified and recertified, as they were mostly malnourished and afraid. While telling the mothers not to give candy to the children, I found myself buying fruit drops to give the children so I could examine them. They would cry, "Mama! She's going to shoot me!" Going into the waiting room, I would take the little one in my arms or hold his hand and take him to the examining room.

First he was weighed with an aide helping to guide his steps. Then his mother would tell, or better yet, we would try to find out from him what he had for breakfast or supper the day before. Then we stressed that it is very important to include milk in all his meals. Then we proceeded to cunningly count his fingers and prick one fingertip for his blood count. This would take about twenty or thirty minutes. After the evaluation, pamphlets were given to the mothers with a complete revision of diet and hygiene if there was evidence of neglect. Some ninety to one hundred and twenty children were seen each week with twenty to thirty expectant mothers. At the medical center work was picking up. The Consulate Missionary Sisters' visits were monthly and welcome.

The girl with whom I shared the trailer was acting up. I had very little use of the bathroom; she would fill the bathtub with her dirty clothes, and the dining table was full of dirty dishes. The drinking water was polluted; when I had it checked, it was found that the cesspool was too near the water supply. That caused confusion with the landlord, who was served notice to build new cesspools. The same worker who picked me up in the morning would bring me tall bottles of well water. The lock on the door was broken. I had to lock myself in my room at nights. Somehow, as time went on, I seemed to be stressed with the difficulties of everyday living.

Meanwhile, at the center, I was seeing some thirty-seven infants a day, many of them screaming. Some sick first aid cases were also brought in. An exceptional case was brought in by the clergy. A thirteen-year-old had a three to four inch lacerated incision of the hand, apparently a day-old accident. The wound and surrounding area was as black as tar.

When I asked what was put on the wound, I was told, "soot, the smoke from the ceiling," was put on to stop the bleeding. I cleaned the wound as much as I could and decided to refer the lad to a nearby hospital emergency room. Well, what do you know, the hospital called me to find out who was going to pay for the service since the parents were unable to. I replied that's simple enough, as far as I know that is where the state steps in. They, however, treated the child and sent him back to the clinic for follow-up until the stitches were ready to be removed.

Time was spent organizing and taking inventory of supplies and equipment that served as an orientation both for me and the new aide. May was Blood Pressure month. Posters were made and put up at various shops and public places. On these days, three each week, we would see from fifty to one hundred patients a day, referring six to eight to their doctor and advising others to be careful.

There was a community holding a carnival, so we went to the area shopkeeper and asked permission to put up a poster. Such carrying on was never seen before at the center. When we returned and told them, we were condemned and outreach workers refused to go, saying it was a white community. I went everywhere. I told them that blood pressure has no color. The director of the center told me I could go anywhere I felt needed us.

Early that Saturday morning, my assistant picked me up and off we went and set up our table and chairs on the show grounds. No sooner were we set up then people started coming in. They were refreshingly different and offered us money that we refused, saying the service was a free courtesy and being done by the medical center for all in the neighborhood. Others offered coffee. In four hours we were seeing some nine or ten an hour and referred nine to see their doctors. When we were nearly through, the other outreach workers, the ones who should have been there to help us set up, appeared. This they purposely did because they knew it was Saturday and we were scheduled to leave at noon. This outreach work served as a closer link with the community; folks returned to thank us over and over again. It was a strange and different world for me.

The nearest public telephone was four to six miles away. The way I could communicate with my folks other than by writing letters, was to go to the retired teacher's home five houses from my trailer to make calls, with the agreement that I pay when she got the bill, since they were all long distance. There was no privacy there, but at least there was the satisfaction of talking to someone of my own. My sisters sometimes called me at the center. Then the director would remark, "Had you been overseas, they would not have been able to call you." Of course, I said the distance would make a difference.

There were days when no one could get fresh vegetables. The Episcopalian clergy who, by the way, was the policeman, district constable, would come to my gate and bring me a supply from his garden and eggs from his own chickens.

The retired teacher demonstrated her friendship in many ways. She would pick me up in her Lincoln, take me shopping, show me her garden, and let me pick some of her beans and corn, and take me to the Gainesville lock and dam, Tombigbee River. If you ever go to Atlanta, please go and take in the breathtaking scenery.

I did my homework under great stress and was at the point of breaking down when I could take it no more. I complained to the director who blamed me for keeping it a secret. There were all sorts of men visiting the place and I started to feel afraid. It became worse when the person with whom I shared the trailer came home one evening, picked up her laundry and was taken by a man to the laundry miles away. And then she told me when a man came and asked for her, I should let him in and entertain him until she returned. I walked down to the retired teacher's house and stayed there until I felt she would be back from the laundry. But to tell the truth, I did not sleep that night for I started to think and to say to myself, that is why the lock on the front door was broken.

A few days before a man came to the gate to beg ice. I brought it out to him. No sooner had he gotten it home, he came back for more. This time he was inside the gate, so I politely told him I had no more for today. Luckily I did not let him in, for afterwards I was told he was a man who had served time in jail for having taken part in a murder.

Hazel McShane

The director was amazed at my stories, and to top it off, there was Hurricane Frederick. The retired schoolteacher always stopped to see how I was getting along, and the Reverend Father, District Constable, preached the next Sunday after the flood with heartfelt expressions of sympathy for the victims of the flood and their relatives.

Shortly after I started, I had met Mr. P, a well-built man and the chief recruiting officer of the national volunteers of the peace corps in Atlanta. He embraced me with open arms and welcomed me to the services I would have to undertake. When he heard of all that was going on, he telephoned me and was by the center to see me the next day. A record was kept of the daily activities of the center, with a monthly summary sent to my director.

We became involved with an elderly lady, crippled with arthritis and high blood pressure, who lived alone, but she was able to move around and help herself in her home. We dusted, swept and even helped to prepare her meals. At times we combed her matted hair, checked her blood pressure, and advised her on medications. This was quite a problem because Auntie (so we called her) had all her medication poured together into one bottle. She said it made it easier for her as the bottles had safety caps. We went to work as soon as we got to the center, called the drugstore, explained the situation, and traveled the thirty-seven miles to secure the right caps for the bottles.

Meanwhile it was arranged that I would get settled into another place. It so happened I was moved into the trailer next to the one where I formerly lived by the director and his helper. I called Mr. P and the local volunteer who picked me up. The director came up in the morning.

It was a day of hard labor for me, washing the floors, walls and windows; the scrubbing and cleaning took quite a while. I planted petunias in front to make a better appearance. The landlord remarked how he wished everybody would do the same to make the place beautiful.

In my own trailer, I felt free to do whatever I wanted. The girl with whom I shared the other trailer did not like my moving. The next morning she came to the trailer to ask for the key. I was afraid to let her in. I told her I would give it to the landlord as my rent was not up and I still had some things left in the trailer. That was the last I saw of her.

I felt free to organize a class in my trailer for mothers and young folks of the district who were interested in learning to knit, crochet, or do tatting. My first meeting went well. I provided cookies, coffee cake, and coffee, and six people came. The second month only three, and the next month only one showed up. The folks claimed they did not have the time to spare. The second month I met all the members of the Board, or the Board members met me, as it appeared everyone was curious to find out all they could about me. They ended up saying they were satisfied and wished me a happy year with the co-op.

There was a lot to be desired at the center. When I got there the doctor had been asked to leave and so the nurse had full responsibility for medical care.

We had one regular gentleman who came to have his varicose ulcers dressed. He had a happy face, but he needed care. Personal advice was given to him and the caretaker provided him with meals. One regular man, a cowboy in his early days and a retired army officer, came to have his blood pressure taken once a month. Other than that, most assignments for visits were given by the clerk to prenatal and postpartum mothers, and to children who were either certified or recertified in the W. I. C. program.

First aids were given quick and efficient treatment, then referred to the nearest hospital or doctor. People came to my home if they needed help. It was a Saturday evening when the Reverend Father came to get me to see a woman who was in labor. I palpated her and told her she had time to get to the hospital to have her baby. Another mother came to my home with a six-month-old with a temperature of one hundred and three degrees. She was sent to the hospital.

Terrible rain and a tornado hit the town. I trembled with fear in the trailer that seemed ready to fall apart. One room was flooded out. I was picked up by the center's handyman that morning as my outreach worker could not cross the road in her car. Very few of us reported for work that day. When I reached the center, two examining rooms were flooded out. It took us days to dry up and get back in shape again.

During this frightening time, two young men were drowned and one escaped when their boat overturned on the river. The whole village was in a state of shock. It was also during this time that I discovered two cases of chicken pox among the children and had them examined by the doctor for confirmation.

The time was right for trying to reach the flood victims; some roads were still unpassable. One house with eight residents, including an infant, had only one room in which they could sleep, and the windows and doors were blown down or broken out.

The consulate nuns from Eutaw were frequent visitors to the center and brought some of their useful goods to leave with us for distribution. One Saturday it was arranged between us that I would be picked up by the nuns and they would take me to this house, desperate for attention. The nuns measured the windows and door for screens to keep out the flies and insects, while I counseled the mother and older children in keeping the foodstuff from being contaminated. The government moved in and most victims were assessed and assigned equitable assistance.

There was confusion at the center for a week as to who should take me to and from the center. Most mornings I was late, but since the flood had crippled everything, very few came to the center. I journeyed to Livingston and Selma for in-service training and was scheduled by my supervisor, the man who chewed tobacco and spat all over where he sat or stood. Sometimes he carried a can to spit in.

A group of us journeyed to Tuskegee to a training seminar for the Southern Co-op planning committee. After returning from a three-day seminar, I was taken by a man who did not know left from right. Of course, he made the wrong turn to follow the patrolman to Montgomery South, three miles. Three hours later we had been through Montgomery, Talasse, Percy Hill Road, Mobile, Fairview Avenue, St. Francis Way, and back to Selma. We got messed up along the way. We stopped to change the driver.

We made plans to celebrate the Year of the Child. Invitations were sent to top officials of the state. Preparations were well on the way when I started to feel the effects of stress. I was granted an administrative leave of absence. On seeing my doctor, I was advised to work less days per week and shorter hours.

I called Atlanta to report the doctor's findings and was told I could take off the remainder of the year and return in January to finish my assignment. I still had two months left to serve. I declined to return. An inspector from the W.I.C. program from the State Department paid us a visit during this time and wanted to know what I would do with my time after I was done serving. Several telephone calls were made and finally the Board decided that it was all right for me not to return. Here again I was placed in a position of finding somewhere to stay besides squatting with my sister Lorraine.

I took a studio apartment in Queens rather than return to my home upstate, because it was stripped of everything but the kitchen table and dining chairs. I stayed in Queens for two full months when my other sister decided that her vacant apartment had no tenant and I could get it. I had to ask permission to leave since I had signed a lease. I had to advertise to get someone to take the apartment and take over some of my furniture; the superintendent got the rest. After three months in my sister's apartment, I moved back to my home in Worcester, New York.

There is more yet to tell; the author still lives to be of service to those in need, not forgetting to thank the Lord.

Hazel McShane